THE D-DAY LANDINGS

Published by IWM, Lambeth Road, London SE1 6HZ
iwm.org.uk

ISBN 978-1-912423-73-6

A catalogue record for this book is available from the British Library
Printed and bound by Gomer Press Limited
Colour reproduction by Zebra

Every effort has been made to contact all copyright holders.
The publishers will be glad to make good in future editions
any error or omissions brought to their attention.

Front cover: 1st Special Service Brigade commandos wade ashore on
Queen Red, Sword beach (detail).

Back cover: Men of No. 4 Commando, 1st Special Service Brigade,
commencing their advance inland from Sword beach (detail).

THE D-DAY LANDINGS

Stephen Walton

Troops of No. 4 Commando and tanks of the Royal Hussars advance along a street in Ouistreham, Sword beach. The image is a still from original wartime footage.

The D-Day landings of 6 June 1944 have become a key part of the collective memory of the Second World War, particularly in Britain, the United States and Canada. They constituted the largest amphibious assault ever undertaken in the history of conflict, which led directly to the defeat of Nazi Germany less than a year later.

Ever since the evacuation of the British Expeditionary Force from Dunkirk in the early summer of 1940, British Prime Minister Winston Churchill had been looking to the day when Britain could return to Nazi-occupied Europe to bring the war to a successful conclusion. He knew that this could not be done without substantial help, mainly from the USA with its vast potential resources. Following America's entry into the war in December 1941, this became a realistic prospect. But it would take time to build up the forces required to launch a successful head-on assault on Adolf Hitler's 'Fortress Europe', particularly given America's substantial commitments in the Pacific against Japan.

In the meantime, Churchill pushed through his alternative strategy of attacking what he called the 'soft underbelly' of the Mediterranean. This involved major Anglo-American amphibious assaults in North Africa and Italy in 1942 and 1943, culminating in the fall of Hitler's Fascist ally Benito Mussolini. The risks of landing on strongly defended enemy shores were cruelly highlighted in the disastrous Dieppe Raid of August 1942, when a large Anglo-Canadian raiding force was decimated on the beaches of northern France. These experiences, good and bad, provided valuable lessons for the future.

Plans for an Allied invasion of north-west Europe proceeded apace during 1943. By the end of the year, Operation 'Overlord' was fully worked out and set to take place in May 1944. US General Dwight Eisenhower was appointed Allied Supreme Commander for this undertaking. The initial assault phase, codenamed 'Neptune', was devised by Eisenhower's designated (British) land, sea and air commanders: General Sir Bernard Law Montgomery, Admiral Sir Bertram Ramsay and Air Marshal Sir Trafford Leigh-Mallory respectively. The success or failure of the amphibious assault on the Normandy beaches in France was largely in the hands of Ramsay, who was responsible for the crucial naval component of 'Neptune', and the real mastermind behind the D-Day landings. He was a veteran of previous amphibious operations and had a genius for the organisation of large forces, so the chances of success were high.

Finally set for 5 June 1944, D-Day suffered a last-minute delay due to bad weather, commencing at last in the early hours of Tuesday 6 June. In accordance with the 'Neptune' plan, British and American airborne troops were first dropped on either flank of the invasion area to secure key objectives ahead of the main amphibious assault. After a massive naval bombardment of German defences along the coast, the British, American and Canadian troops of Montgomery's 21st Army Group went ashore in their designated landing sectors, codenamed Utah, Omaha, Gold, Juno and Sword. Around 156,000 troops were landed on D-Day alone, a remarkable feat by any standard. By the early afternoon, the Allies were firmly established in the assault area, with British forces beginning the advance inland towards Caen. Many difficult and costly months of fighting lay ahead, but the crucial first step had been taken.

The German response to these events was severely

compromised by several factors. Field Marshal Erwin Rommel, commander of Army Group B, which was the first line of defence in Normandy, disagreed fundamentally with his superior, Commander-in-Chief West Gerd von Rundstedt, on the strategy to be adopted to meet the expected invasion. As a result, their forces were divided and ill-prepared to react effectively. Unpredictable and poorly informed interventions by Hitler further complicated the situation. The much-vaunted system of fixed defences known as the 'Atlantic Wall' was insufficiently manned and offered little real resistance. Substantial German forces were also held back from the invasion area in the belief (encouraged by elaborate Allied deception measures) that the main blow would fall elsewhere, most likely in the Pas-de-Calais further east. Hitler's armed forces were in any case exhausted by the colossal war of attrition on the Eastern Front and had little spare capacity to deal with the 'second front' which had now opened up in the west. Operation 'Bagration', a massive Soviet offensive in the Byelorussian sector, was timed to coincide with the opening of the Normandy campaign, obliging Hitler to respond to two major Allied offensives at the same time. The fate of the Third Reich was effectively sealed.

The momentous events of D-Day were captured on camera by a relative handful of British (notably No. 5 Army Film and Photographic Unit), American and Canadian cameramen attached to the Allied armies, navies and air forces – probably fewer than 50 of them altogether. They were exposed to the same dangers and hardships as the soldiers, sailors and airmen they worked alongside. This book contains a small selection of the many hundreds of powerful images they took on that day, as well as those taken during the lead-up to D-Day, which are part of the IWM Photograph Archive.

A road 'somewhere in England' lined with metal shelters containing artillery shells, photographed in the months before D-Day. As part of the preparations for the Normandy landings, vast quantities of ammunition were stockpiled at locations across the country. From the air, these shelters would have looked like agricultural structures.

Pontoon bridge components at a supply depot in southern England, awaiting issue to army engineer units prior to D-Day. Everything had to be ready to enable the invasion force to progress rapidly beyond the Normandy beaches, further into northern France.

Concrete caissons under construction at Surrey Docks in London, April 1944. These formed part of the artificial 'Mulberry' harbours that were towed across the English Channel after D-Day to facilitate supplies and reinforcements, before ports such as Cherbourg could be secured.

American soldiers file into a briefing tent in one of the many sealed-off and closely guarded assembly areas near the south coast of England, May 1944. Around one and a half million US troops were stationed in England at this time to participate in the Normandy campaign.

British soldiers learn to swim across a waterway in full kit during an army training course, May 1944. The risk of drowning was just one of the many hazards faced by men of an amphibious assault force.

Railway yards at Tourcoing in northern France being bombed by the Royal Air Force (RAF) a month before D-Day. Disrupting the transport network that would enable the Germans to move men and equipment up to the Normandy battlefields was a key objective of the Allies ahead of the landings.

A street scene in Southampton on the eve of D-Day. Members of the Bagg family go about their domestic chores as an American artillery unit parked in the road makes preparations for its deployment to Normandy. A major part of the initial invasion fleet sailed from Southampton.

An American soldier surrounded by arms and equipment waits in a landing craft for the Normandy invasion to begin. To his left is his anti-tank rocket launcher, popularly known as the 'bazooka'. At his right is a pole charge for clearing obstacles at close quarters.

US Navy LCTs (Landing Craft Tank) at Portland, fully loaded with men and vehicles waiting for the crossing to Normandy. They are part of Assault Force O, which assembled there and at Weymouth, destined for Omaha beach.

German beach obstacles in the Gold area. Rommel had thousands of such obstacles placed along the Normandy coast to hinder a seaborne assault, as part of the Atlantic Wall defences. These 'hedgehogs', designed to impale and disable landing craft, have been exposed at low tide.

Major General Richard Gale, Commander of the British 6th Airborne Division, talking with paratroopers at RAF Harwell, Oxfordshire, on the eve of D-Day. 6th Airborne was tasked with securing the left flank of the Allied assault area before the troops stormed the beaches.

Officers of 22nd Independent Parachute Company, 6th Airborne Division, synchronise their watches for the start of D-Day. They were among the first Allied troops to land in Normandy; their job was to mark out the landing zones ahead of the arrival of the main 6th Airborne force. Officers named (from left to right): Lieutenants Robert de Lautour, Don Wells, John Vischer and Bob Midwood.

4007   16/412-6JUN44:20//K18.

6th Airborne Division troops beside their Horsa which has crashed through a wall on landing, near Ranville. Britain's primary combat glider, and made largely of wood, the Airspeed Horsa enabled groups of men and equipment to land in one place, rather than being scattered by airdrop.

An aerial photograph showing Airspeed Horsa gliders of 6th Airborne Division after landing by the Caen Canal at Bénouville. The bridge, top left, became famous as 'Pegasus Bridge', the first British objective to be captured on D-Day, seized by men of the Oxfordshire and Buckinghamshire Light Infantry under Major John Howard.

General Dwight Eisenhower, Supreme Allied Commander for Operation 'Overlord', talking with men of the US 101st Airborne Division on the eve of D-Day. Together with the US 82nd Airborne Division, it was responsible for securing the right flank of the seaborne assault force.

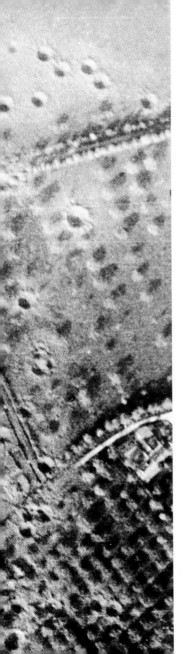

An aerial view of the large German gun battery at Merville, following Allied bombing in the weeks before D-Day. Overlooking Sword beach, it posed a serious threat until it was captured in the early hours of D-Day by British troops of the Parachute Regiment and Royal Marine Commandos.

Men of the British 6th Airlanding Brigade admire graffiti chalked on their Horsa as they emplane for Normandy. It refers to the failure of German plans to invade Britain, codenamed Operation 'Sealion', earlier in the war.

A Horsa of 6th Airlanding Brigade being towed aloft on the evening of 6 June as part of the second major airlift of troops to Normandy on D-Day. It is being pulled by an Armstrong Whitworth Albemarle, one of the RAF's main glider tugs and paratroop transporters.

6th Airborne Division gliders scattered over part of Drop Zone N east of the Orne River. The upper half of the photograph shows the typical Normandy bocage country, which posed serious challenges for the Allied advance inland, with its dense hedgerows providing ideal cover for the German defenders.

Royal Navy sailors, Able Seaman Joseph Adams and
Leading Seaman Charles Fagg, on board the frigate
HMS *Holmes* reading Eisenhower's 'Order of the Day'
for the Normandy invasion. *Holmes* was part of the
escort for Bombarding Force D off Le Havre, which
provided naval firepower in support of the troops
going ashore on Sword beach.

The British battleship HMS *Ramillies* during a heavy bombardment of German coastal defences in the Sword area. Almost 7,000 Allied ships and 25,000 Allied sailors were involved in the D-Day landing operations.

A US Army chaplain, Father (Major) Edward Waters, conducts a service for American soldiers and sailors about to leave Weymouth for the Normandy beaches. Good chaplains were much respected in their units, sharing the dangers and hardships besides providing consolation and burying the dead.

The bodies of American soldiers lie by the water's edge on Omaha beach. 'Bloody Omaha' was the most heavily defended of the Allied landing beaches, with seasoned troops of the German 352nd Infantry Division inflicting a large number of casualties.

Heavily laden follow-up troops from the US 1st Infantry Division disembark onto the Easy Red sector of Omaha beach. Amphibious vehicles (including two DUKW 'Duck' trucks) and towed artillery can be seen, with lines of soldiers moving inland beyond.

The scene on Omaha beach after the initial landings, with naval support vessels massed offshore and LSTs (Landing Ship Tank) unloading directly onto the beach. Barrage balloons are deployed to deter low-level German air attacks.

A soldier of the US Army Medical Corps tends to a wounded colleague on Utah beach. They are serving with the US 4th Infantry Division, which went on to play a prominent part in the capture of the port of Cherbourg, a prime 'Overlord' objective.

Troops of the US VII Corps shelter in front of the sea wall in the Uncle Red sector, Utah beach, with others starting the advance beyond it. Utah was relatively lightly defended, in sharp contrast to Omaha, although the advance to Cherbourg was hindered by difficult terrain.

Men and vehicles of 168 (City of London) Light Field Ambulance, Royal Army Medical Corps, on the approach to Gold beach. There were over 10,000 Allied casualties on D-Day, those killed in action making up just under half of the total.

British 50th (Northumbrian) Infantry Division troops coming ashore on Gold beach, many equipped with bicycles. The British and Canadians made extensive use of the military-issue bicycle, including folding models, although during amphibious landings they could be more of a hindrance.

Sherman tanks of the Nottinghamshire
Yeomanry driving off a landing craft onto Gold
beach, as a bulldozer clears a path across
the sand. Although difficult to get ashore,
bulldozers played a vital role during D-Day in
literally smoothing the way for other vehicles.
Eisenhower considered them to be one of the
most significant weapons of the war.

1st Special Service Brigade commandos wade ashore on Queen Red, Sword beach, led by Brigadier Simon Fraser (Lord Lovat) who can be seen in the water to the right of his men. Directly in front of the camera is Lovat's personal bagpiper, Bill Millin, playing rousing tunes as he disembarks.

The view from LCT 610 during the initial assault on the Queen Red sector, Sword beach. Anti-landing obstacles can be seen protruding from the water, while a tank burns on the beach. Casualties on Queen Red were among the heaviest suffered by the British during the day.

German prisoners of war (POWs) being marched away from Sword beach. Many of the Atlantic Wall defenders first encountered by the Allies were inexperienced and demoralised, considering themselves fortunate to be captured rather than killed.

Men of No. 4 Commando, 1st Special Service Brigade, commencing their advance inland from Sword beach. In the background a converted Churchill tank AVRE (Armoured Vehicle Royal Engineers) carries a folding bridge.

British dead lie alongside abandoned equipment in front of German 'resistance nest' (*Widerstandsnest*) WN 20, Sword beach. WN 20, codenamed 'Cod' by the Allies, was one of a string of such defensive strongpoints built along the coast as part of the Atlantic Wall, and caused many casualties on D-Day.

The cruiser HMS *Belfast* leads Bombarding Force E in support of the Juno landings. Juno was the 'Canadian beach', allocated to the Canadian 3rd Infantry Division and 2nd Armoured Brigade, with more than 21,000 troops going ashore by the end of the day.

Smoke rising from burning buildings in Bernières-sur-Mer in the Juno area, as a result of the preceding naval bombardments. Rough seas and strong German defences made it a difficult objective for the Canadian troops who saw this scene from their landing craft.

Soldiers of the North Shore (New Brunswick) Regiment exit their landing craft at Saint-Aubin-sur-Mer, Juno beach, under fire from German troops in the abandoned houses opposite. The image is a still from the British-American 1945 documentary film *The True Glory*, using original wartime footage.

Men of B Company, North Shore (New Brunswick) Regiment, take cover on the approach to German strongpoint WN 27 at Saint-Aubin-sur-Mer. The regiment captured it in less than two hours after setting foot on the beaches.

Wrecked landing craft in the Nan Red sector of Juno beach. No. 48 Royal Marine Commando, supporting the Canadians, suffered heavy casualties in this area, including two of their landing craft hitting mines offshore. It was a bloody baptism for the unit, which had only been raised in March 1944.

Troops of No. 4 Commando and tanks of the Royal Hussars advance along a street in Ouistreham, Sword beach. The tanks are modified 'duplex drive' (DD) Shermans, fitted with propulsion screws and inflatable rubber skirts to facilitate their use in amphibious operations. The image is a still from original wartime footage.

1st Special Service Brigade commandos in action with a Bren light machine gun. Having taken Ouistreham, their task was to link up with and relieve troops of 6th Airborne Division at Bénouville on the Caen Canal. The city of Caen was the main British objective on D-Day.

A British soldier inspects a German Goliath remote-controlled demolition vehicle, Sword beach. Designed to destroy a variety of targets including buildings, tanks and troop concentrations, the Goliath was deployed by the Germans on all fighting fronts, including the Atlantic Wall, but to little effect.

Men of 50th (Northumbrian) Division looking at a knocked-out German gun emplacement, Gold beach. A typical component of the Atlantic Wall, construction of which started in 1942 and eventually extended for over 1,600 miles from the Spanish border to northern Norway, to deter or repel Allied seaborne attacks from British soil.

British soldiers sharing mugs of cocoa with a French boy in Ver-sur-Mer, Gold beach. The Allies mostly received a warm welcome from the local population, but there was also fear, suspicion and hostility from some whose homes and livelihoods had been destroyed by war.

British commandos marching German and Italian POWs to the rear, Sword area. The Allies encountered several nationalities serving with the German forces in Normandy, mainly Soviet and Eastern European, these Italians may have been part of an Atlantic Wall labour battalion.

Inhabitants of La Brèche d'Hermanville, Sword beach, have their identity papers checked by an officer of the Royal Army Service Corps. French civilians were subject to numerous restrictions and regulations by the Allies, including travel permits and curfews, dictated by military priorities.

British carrier pigeon Gustav, who brought the first news report of D-Day back from the invasion fleet off the Normandy coast. Carrier pigeons played a vital role in wartime communications, in this case where radio silence was in force, and Gustav was awarded the PDSA Dickin Medal (the 'animal Victoria Cross') for his services.

A rare colour photograph, showing North American P-51 Mustangs of 361st Fighter Group (US Eighth Air Force) preparing to take off for Normandy from RAF Bottisham, Cambridgeshire. Allied fighter and bomber aircraft flew over 10,000 sorties in support of the initial landings.

German POWs tending an American cemetery at St Laurent, near Omaha beach, June 1945. It was established by the US First Army two days after D-Day, and is now the Normandy American Cemetery containing the graves of over 9,000 war dead from that period.

Image List

MH 2012 (detail), AP 15665, EA 22916, H 37607, EA 25409, H 38125, C 4399, NYT 27247, PL 25481, EA 13138, A 23992, H 39068, H 39070, MH 2074, B 5050, EA 25491, MH 24804, H 39178, H 39183, MH 2076, A 23926, A 24459, EA 25518, EA 25734, EA 25644, EA 26941, OWIL 44977, EA 25902, A 23890, B 5261, B 5259, B 5111, B 5103, B 5079, B 5071, B 5118, HU 65360, A 23934, IWM FLM 2570, B 5228, B 5225, MH 2012, B 5057, B 5115, B 5252, B 5254, B 5042, B 5059, CH 13321, FRE 6207, FRA 107170

About the Author

Stephen Walton is a Senior Curator in the Second World War & Mid-20th Century Conflict Team and is based at IWM Duxford. He joined IWM in 1990 as an Archivist, working on the museum's extensive collections of letters, diaries, unpublished memoirs and other documents of service personnel and civilians during both World Wars. Areas of current interest include the Second World War from the German perspective and the war in South East Asia.

Acknowledgements

The author would like to thank IWM colleagues Lara Bateman (Publishing Officer), James Taylor (Principal Curator, Public History) and Helen Mavin (Head of Photographs) for their help with this publication. My Second World War Team colleague Adrian Kerrison provided useful advice and information on a number of the images which appear in the book.